Nearest to the Sun

The Planet Mercury

by Nancy Loewen   illustrated by Jeff Yesh

PICTURE WINDOW BOOKS
Minneapolis, Minnesota

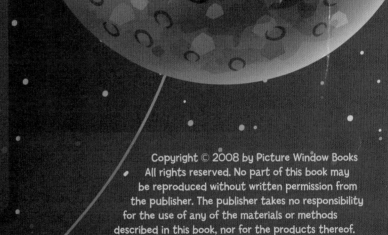

Thanks to our advisers for their expertise, research, and advice:

Lynne Hillenbrand, Ph.D., Professor of Astronomy
California Institute of Technology

Terry Flaherty, Ph.D., Professor of English
Minnesota State University, Mankato

Editor: Jill Kalz
Designers: Amy Muehlenhardt and Melissa Kes
Page Production: Melissa Kes
Art Director: Nathan Gassman
Associate Managing Editor: Christianne Jones
The illustrations in this book were created digitally.

Picture Window Books
5115 Excelsior Boulevard
Suite 232
Minneapolis, MN 55416
877-845-8392
www.picturewindowbooks.com

Printed in the United States of America.

 All books published by Picture Window Books
are manufactured with paper containing at least
10 percent post-consumer waste.

Library of Congress Cataloging-in-Publication Data
Loewen, Nancy, 1964-
Nearest to the sun : the planet Mercury / by Nancy Loewen ; illustrated by
Jeff Yesh.
p. cm. — (Amazing science. Planets)
Includes index.
ISBN: 978-1-4048-3954-0 (library binding)
ISBN: 978-1-4048-3963-2 (paperback)
1. Mercury (Planet)—Juvenile literature. I. Yesh, Jeff, 1971- ill. II. Title.
QB611.L64 2008
523.41—dc22   2007032876

Table of Contents

A Strange Sunrise

Imagine that you're standing on the planet Mercury. It's morning. The sun is rising. But you've never seen a sunrise like this one. The sun appears two and a half times as large as it does on Earth. Yet the sky stays black!

And what's this? The sun has risen halfway up the sky, but now it's going back down. It dips below the horizon. Wait—now it's rising again! How strange!

FUN FACT

The planet Mercury was named after a quick-footed Roman god.

The Fastest Planet

Mercury is the fastest planet. It zips through space at about 30 miles (48 kilometers) per second. Mercury completes its orbit around the sun (what we call one year) in about 88 Earth days.

Mercury's path is oval shaped, like an egg. Because of this shape, Mercury speeds up and slows down at different places in its orbit. Other planets follow an almost circular path around the sun.

Jupiter

Uranus

Neptune

Saturn

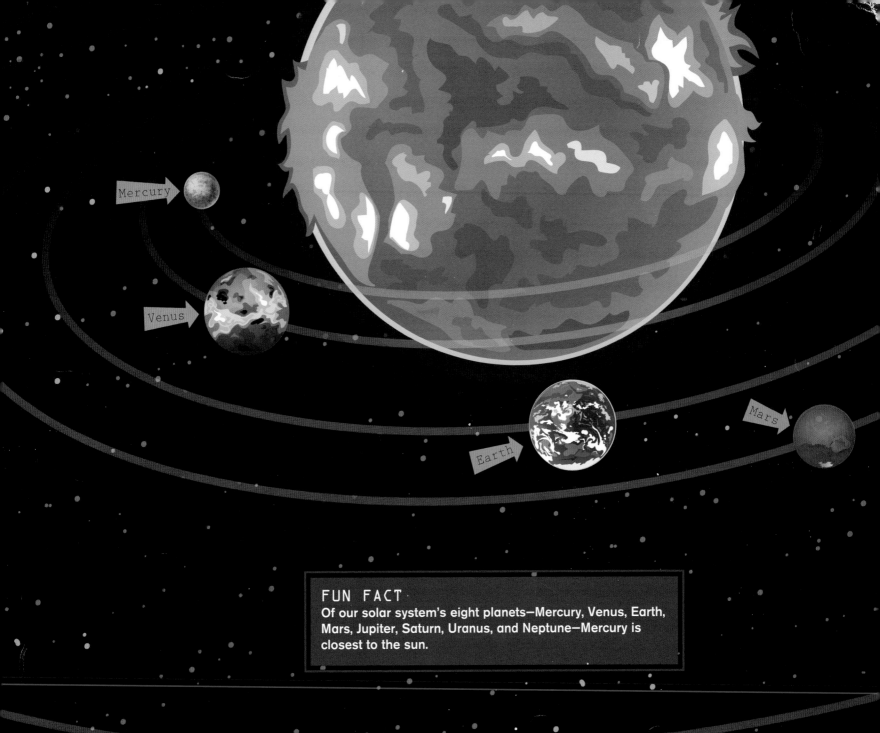

FUN FACT

Of our solar system's eight planets—Mercury, Venus, Earth, Mars, Jupiter, Saturn, Uranus, and Neptune—Mercury is closest to the sun.

EDITOR'S NOTE:

In this illustration, the distances between planets are not to scale. In reality, the distances between the outer planets are much greater than the distances between the inner planets.

Spinning Slowly

Mercury has a short year, but it has a very long day. It takes Earth 24 hours to spin on its axis one time (what we call one day). It takes Mercury 59 Earth days to spin on its axis one time.

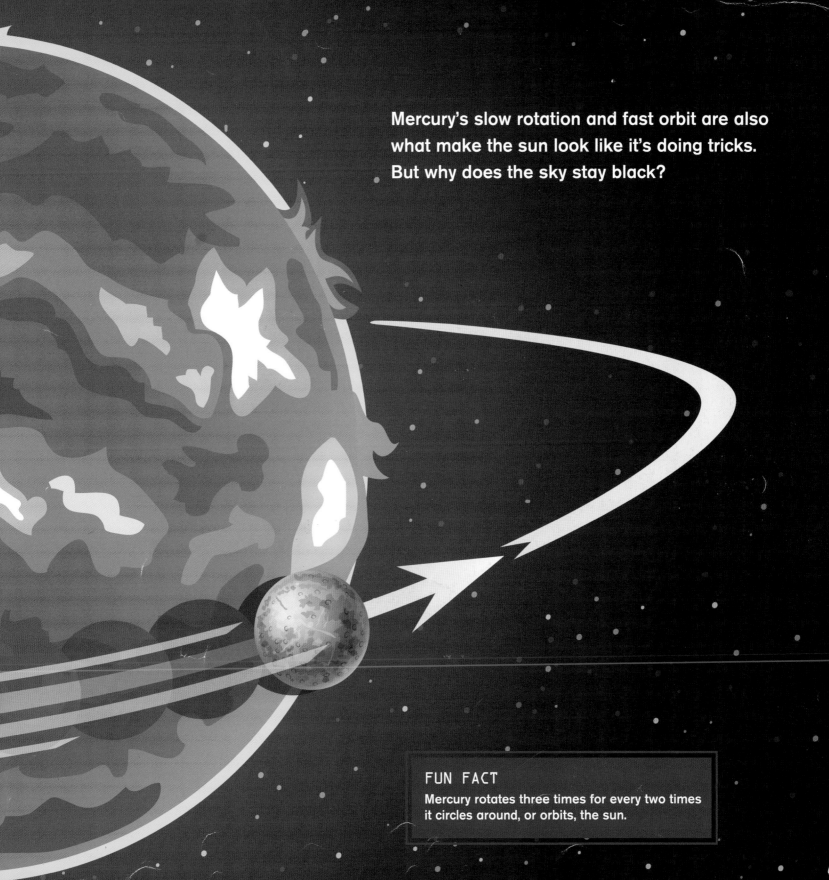

Mercury's slow rotation and fast orbit are also what make the sun look like it's doing tricks. But why does the sky stay black?

FUN FACT

Mercury rotates three times for every two times it circles around, or orbits, the sun.

A Bare Planet

Most planets are wrapped in a layer of gases called an atmosphere. On Earth, sunlight enters the atmosphere and makes the sky appear blue.

But Mercury has almost no atmosphere. That's why the sky always appears black.

FUN FACT
Mercury is tilted only slightly on its axis. As a result, the planet receives the same amount of sunlight all year long.

Hot and Cold

Without an atmosphere to screen the sun's rays, Mercury gets very hot during the day. Temperatures reach 800 degrees Fahrenheit (427 degrees Celsius).

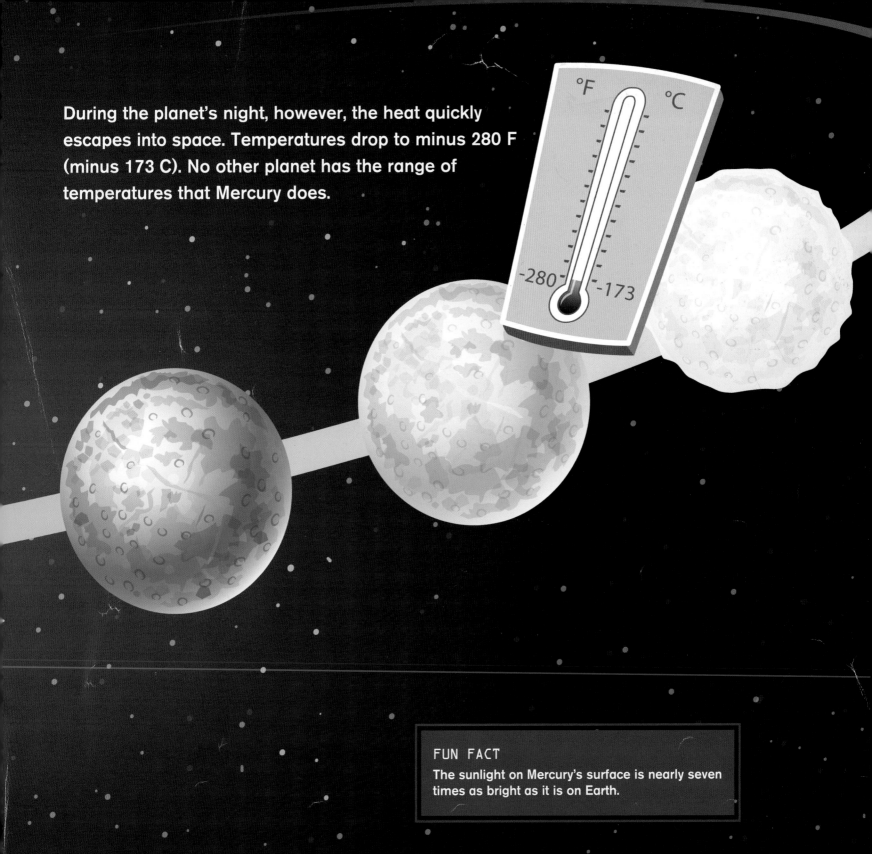

During the planet's night, however, the heat quickly escapes into space. Temperatures drop to minus 280 F (minus 173 C). No other planet has the range of temperatures that Mercury does.

FUN FACT

The sunlight on Mercury's surface is nearly seven times as bright as it is on Earth.

The Smallest Planet

Mercury is the smallest planet in our solar system. Its diameter is two and a half times less than Earth's.

Earth

Mercury

Many scientists believe that at one time, Mercury was much larger. A giant asteroid may have hit Mercury and broken apart its outer layer of rock.

FUN FACT

Mercury has a large iron core, or center. The core is about 42 percent of the planet's size.

Crater City

Mercury is close in size to our moon. Its surface is similar to the moon's, too. It is covered with craters. A crater is a bowl-shaped hole that is made by a hard object hitting the surface.

Usually, a planet's atmosphere slows down any flying objects. Smaller objects might burn up in the atmosphere and never reach the surface at all. But that doesn't happen on Mercury. Flying objects hit the surface at full speed.

FUN FACT

There is no wind or rain on Mercury. As a result, craters never wear down.

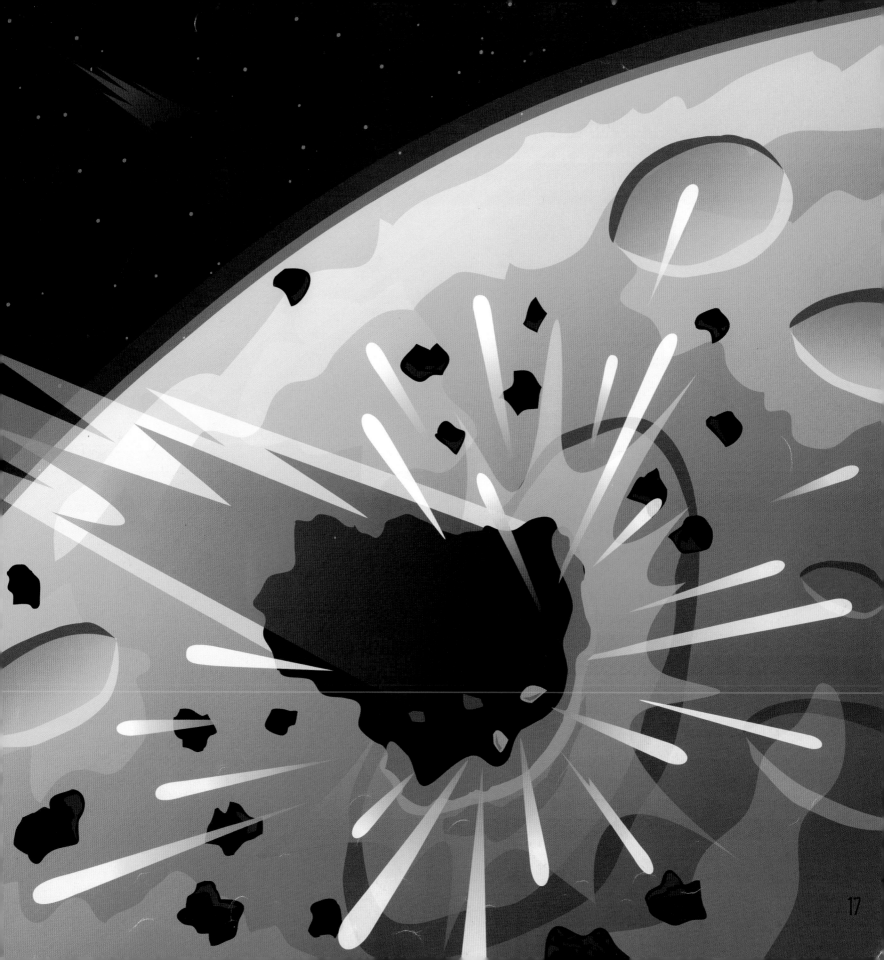

Mercury has one of the largest craters in the entire solar system. The Caloris Basin is 806 miles (1,290 km) wide. The crash that formed the crater was so powerful that it caused lava explosions. It even created hills on the opposite side of the planet.

FUN FACT
Besides craters, Mercury also has mountains, plains, and valleys.

Much to Discover

Because of its position near the sun, Mercury has been difficult for scientists to study. Only one spacecraft has visited the planet. The *Mariner 10* flew by three times in 1974 and 1975.

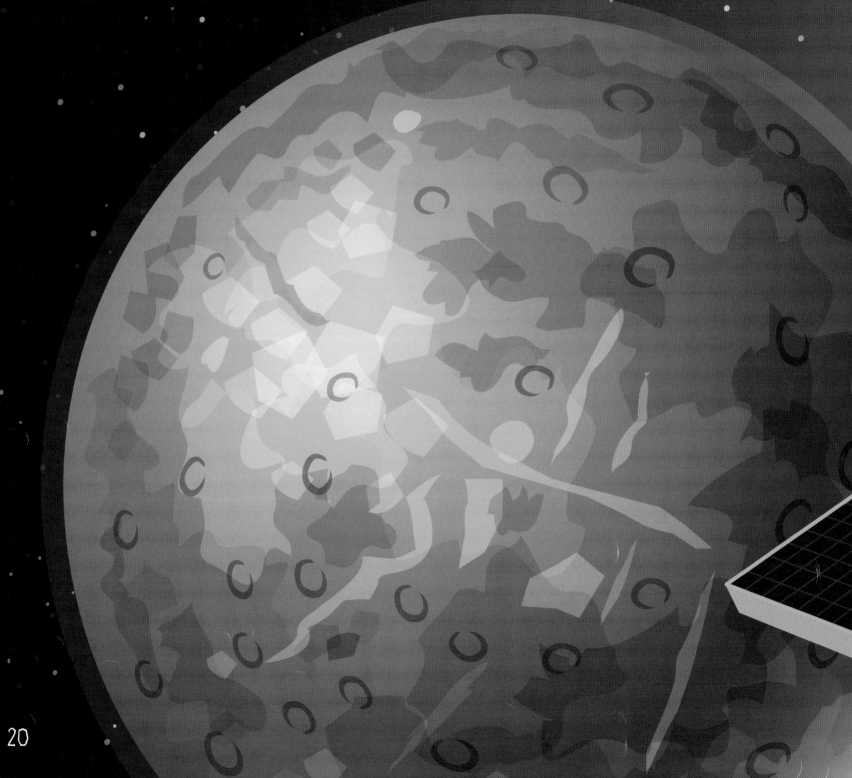

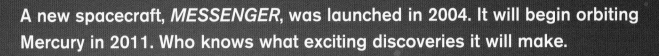

A new spacecraft, *MESSENGER*, was launched in 2004. It will begin orbiting Mercury in 2011. Who knows what exciting discoveries it will make.

FUN FACT

MESSENGER stands for *ME*rcury *S*urface, *S*pace *EN*vironment, *GE*ochemistry, and *R*anging.

Making Craters

What you need:

- a small rubber ball
- two trays, box lids, or baking pans with edges
- flour (sand will work, too)

What you do:

1. Go outside and fill the trays with flour. The flour should be at least 1 inch (2.5 centimeters) thick.

2. Stand above one tray and drop the ball into the flour. Remove the ball and look at your crater. How big is it?

3. Now stand above the other tray. This time, don't drop the ball; throw it down hard! Remove the ball. How does this crater compare to the first one? How is this like what happens on Mercury?

Fun Facts

- Mercury doesn't have any moons.

- Mercury is one of the four terrestrial planets, along with Venus, Earth, and Mars. These planets are made of rock. Jupiter, Saturn, Uranus, and Neptune are gas giant planets. They are made mostly of gases and are far bigger than terrestrial planets.

- Mercury's gravity is about 39 percent of Earth's. If you weigh 100 pounds (45 kilograms) on Earth, you would weigh 39 pounds (18 kg) on Mercury.

- From Earth, Mercury can be seen only at twilight or at dawn. It never gets very high in the sky.

Glossary

asteroid—a rock that circles around the sun

atmosphere—the gases that surround a planet

axis—the center on which something spins, or rotates

diameter—the distance of a line running from one side of a circle, through the center, and across to the other side

gravity—the force that pulls things down toward the surface of a planet

horizon—the area where a planet's surface appears to meet the sky

lava—molten (melted) rock that comes from inside a planet

orbit—the path an object takes to travel around a star or planet; also, to travel around a star or planet

rotation—to complete a circle on an axis or center

solar system—the sun and the bodies that orbit around it; these bodies include planets, dwarf planets, asteroids, and comets

To Learn More

More Books to Read

Asimov, Isaac, with revisions and updating by Richard Hantula. *Mercury.* Milwaukee: Gareth Stevens Pub., 2002.

Rau, Dana Meachen. *Mercury.* Minneapolis: Compass Point Books, 2002.

Stille, Darlene. *Mercury.* Chanhassen, Minn.: Child's World, 2004.

On the Web

FactHound offers a safe, fun way to find Web sites related to topics in this book. All of the sites on FactHound have been researched by our staff.

1. Visit *www.facthound.com*
2. Type in this special code: 1404839542
3. Click on the FETCH IT button.

Your trusty FactHound will fetch the best sites for you!

Index

Look for all of the books in the Amazing Science: Planets series:

Brightest in the Sky: The Planet Venus
Dwarf Planets: Pluto, Charon, Ceres, and Eris
Farthest from the Sun: The Planet Neptune
The Largest Planet: Jupiter
Nearest to the Sun: The Planet Mercury
Our Home Planet: Earth
Ringed Giant: The Planet Saturn
Seeing Red: The Planet Mars
The Sideways Planet: Uranus